GUYS & Girls:
UNDERSTANDING EACH OTHER

A 4-week course to help junior highers learn how to relate to the opposite sex

by Linda Snyder

Group
Loveland, Colorado

Guys & Girls: Understanding Each Other
Copyright © 1991 by Group Publishing, Inc.

Third Printing, 1993

Credits
Edited by Michael D. Warden
Cover designed by Jill Bendykowski and DeWain Stoll
Interior designed by Judy Atwood Bienick and Jan Aufdemberge
Illustrations by Judy Atwood Bienick

ISBN 1-55945-110-6
Printed in the United States of America

CONTENTS

96510

GUYS & GIRLS: UNDERSTANDING EACH OTHER

It all happened so fast. Suddenly Tim felt ugly and insecure. Everything was different—his body, his thoughts, his reactions. He'd gotten clumsy, tripping over his feet and walking into walls. And hair—it was everywhere now. Worst of all, he'd lost control of his body. His voice cracked just when that cute girl stopped to ask him a question. And when he saw her, he felt things he couldn't explain or stop.

He was on a roller coaster. One minute he felt great and the next he was ready to crawl in a hole and hide. He just didn't understand the changes happening to him. And there was no one he could talk to.

Tim was sure he was the only one who felt that way. He didn't know that every young person in the midst of puberty would've understood.

Puberty is a tough time for guys and girls alike. Guys and girls gradually become aware of each other and begin to feel drawn for no apparent reason. Notice in the chart in the margin how kids' interest in attending parties where there are guys and girls increases from 5th to 9th grade. They're captured by the mystery and excitement of love relationships. But they're not sure how they should relate, what they should say or how they should act. It can be scary.

And often there's no one to help.

We need to prepare young people for adolescence with down-to-earth answers that meet their physical, emotional, intellectual *and* spiritual needs. Junior highers need to know that when their bodies betray them and their emotions confuse them, they're still loved—by God and you.

Percent of kids who like to attend parties or dances where there are guys and girls:

	Guys	Girls
5th-graders	49%	41%
7th-graders	60%	63%
9th-graders	71%	71%

Changes in Puberty

The American School Health Association cites several changes that occur in young people as they go through puberty. Here are some of them.

Physical Characteristics
- Accelerated, uneven growth
- Variable coordination
- Visual problems
- Skin problems
- Voice changes
- Growth of reproductive organs

Emotional Characteristics
- Sudden and deep mood swings
- Strong feelings of like and dislike
- Sensitive or self-critical attitudes
- Stress about physical and emotional changes
- Desire for independence from adults
- Extreme self-consciousness

Social Characteristics
- Feelings of social insecurity
- Need to argue against authority, though they still want it
- New awareness of the opposite sex
- New interest in competitive sports

Intellectual Characteristics
- Greater curiosity and eagerness to learn
- Desire to read more
- Wider range of abilities and interests
- Desire to succeed
- Skeptical attitude, demanding facts
- Need for precise assignments and meaningful experiences

This four-week course will help your junior highers and middle schoolers deal with the confusing, fast-paced changes of puberty. They'll learn how to relate to each other as young men and women. And they'll discover a few more keys to unlock the mystery of the opposite sex.

By the end of this course your students will:
- identify positive childhood qualities and seek to develop new spiritual maturity;
- examine the physical, emotional, intellectual and spiritual changes of puberty;
- recognize their positive qualities and physical assets as they view themselves through God's eyes;
- study how specific Bible characters dealt with fear and insecurity;
- discover the range of their feelings and learn to manage them; and
- explore roles and relationships between men and women.

COURSE OBJECTIVES

HOW TO USE THIS COURSE

ACTIVE LEARNING

Think back on an important lesson you've learned in life. Did you learn it from reading about it? from hearing about it? from something you experienced? Chances are, the most important lessons you've learned came from something you experienced. That's what active learning is—learning by doing. And active learning is a key element in Group's Active Bible Curriculum.

Active learning leads students in doing things that help them understand important principles, messages and ideas. It's a discovery process that helps kids internalize what they learn.

Each lesson section in Group's Active Bible Curriculum plays an important part in active learning:

The **Opener** involves kids in the topic in fun and unusual ways.

The **Action and Reflection** includes an experience designed to evoke specific feelings in the students. This section also processes those feelings through "How did you feel?" questions and applies the message to situations kids face.

The **Bible Application** actively connects the topic with the Bible. It helps kids see how the Bible is relevant to the situations they face.

The **Commitment** helps students internalize the Bible's message and commit to make changes in their lives.

The **Closing** funnels the lesson's message into a time of creative reflection and prayer.

When you put all the sections together, you get a lesson that's fun to teach—and kids get messages they'll remember.

BEFORE THE 4-WEEK SESSION

● Read the Introduction, the Course Objectives and This Course at a Glance.

● Decide how you'll publicize the course using the art on the Publicity Page (p. 9). Prepare fliers, newsletter articles and posters as needed.

● Look at the Bonus Ideas (p. 45) and decide which ones you'll use.

● Read the opening statements, Objectives and Bible Basis for the lesson. The Bible Basis shows how specific passages relate to junior highers and middle schoolers today.

● Choose which Opener and Closing options to use. Each is appropriate for a different kind of group. The first option is often more active.

● Gather necessary supplies from This Lesson at a Glance.

● Read each section of the lesson. Adjust where necessary for your class size and meeting room.

● The approximate minutes listed give you an idea of how long each activity will take. Each lesson is designed to take 35 to 60 minutes. Shorten or lengthen activities as needed to fit your group.

● If you see you're going to have extra time, do an activity or two from the "If You Still Have Time . . ." box or from the Bonus Ideas (p. 45).

● Dive into the activities with the kids. Don't be a spectator. The lesson will be more success-ful and rewarding to you and your students.

BEFORE EACH LESSON

HELPFUL HINTS

● The answers given after discussion ques-tions are responses your students *might* give. They aren't the only answers or the "right" answers. If needed, use them to spark dis-cussion. Kids won't always say what you wish they'd say. That's why some of the responses given are negative or controversial. If some-one responds negatively, don't be shocked. Accept the person, and use the opportunity to explore other angles of the issue.

THIS COURSE AT A GLANCE

Before you dive into the lessons, familiarize yourself with each lesson aim. Then read the scripture passages.
- Study them as a background to the lessons.
- Use them as a basis for your personal devotions.
- Think about how they relate to kids' circumstances today.

LESSON 1: NO MORE TRUCKS AND DOLLS

Lesson Aim: To help junior highers understand the transition from childhood to adulthood.

Bible Basis: Luke 2:41-52 and 2 Peter 1:3-11.

LESSON 2: BODY DIFFERENCES

Lesson Aim: To help junior highers cope with the physical changes of puberty.

Bible Basis: Genesis 1:26-31; Psalm 139:13-16; and Song of Songs 4:1-7; 5:10-16.

LESSON 3: BATTLE OF THE SEXES

Lesson Aim: To help junior highers put sex roles and stereotypes in a Christian perspective.

Bible Basis: Genesis 2:18-25 and Galatians 3:26—4:7.

LESSON 4: UPS AND DOWNS

Lesson Aim: To help junior highers understand the similarities and differences in guys' and girls' emotions.

Bible Basis: Joshua 1:1-11 and Mark 4:35-41.

PUBLICITY PAGE

Grab your junior highers' attention! Copy this page, then cut and paste the art of your choice in your church bulletin or newsletter to advertise this course on getting to know the opposite sex. Or copy and use the ready-made flier as a bulletin insert.

Permission to photocopy clip art is granted for local church use.

Splash this art on posters, fliers or even postcards! Just add the vital details: the date and time the course begins, and where you'll meet.

It's that simple.

GUYS & Girls: UNDERSTANDING EACH OTHER

GUYS & Girls: UNDERSTANDING EACH OTHER

GUYS & Girls: UNDERSTANDING EACH OTHER

A 4-week junior high and middle school course on understanding the opposite sex

Come to _____

On _____

At _____

Come learn how to handle the pressures of growing up.

NO MORE TRUCKS AND DOLLS

Junior highers are caught somewhere between childhood and adulthood. And they often don't know how they're supposed to act. Kids need to know it's okay to struggle with the transition from childhood to adulthood. And by understanding how guys and girls struggle differently, kids can learn to make the transition more smoothly.

To help junior highers understand the transition from childhood to adulthood.

LESSON AIM

Students will:
- **recall their childhood memories;**
- **use statistics to discover "favorite" activities of guys and girls their age;**
- **identify childhood qualities worth keeping; and**
- **examine building blocks for maturing faith.**

OBJECTIVES

Look up the following scriptures. Then read the background paragraphs to see how the passages relate to your junior highers and middle schoolers.

In **Luke 2:41-52**, Jesus goes to Jerusalem as a child to attend the feast of Passover.

At 12 years old, Jesus attended his first Passover feast. When his parents left, Jesus stayed behind without their knowledge to listen to the religious leaders. When his parents came back for him, Jesus obeyed them.

Teenagers have a built-in role model in the child Jesus.

BIBLE BASIS
LUKE 2:41-52
2 PETER 1:3-11

Even God's son took time to search for spiritual knowledge. And even knowing he was the Son of God, Jesus remained humble and obedient to his earthly parents. Kids can gain insight from Jesus' quest for knowledge and his respect for his parents.

In **2 Peter 1:3-11**, Peter outlines steps to maturity in Christ.

Peter teaches that a Christian validates his or her call from God by growing toward maturity in Christian qualities. He lists several qualities to be added one on top of the other if Christians are to grow in their faith.

Kids can learn that there's more to growing up than height charts and driver's licenses. They can examine Christian qualities and see how striving after them will make kids more productive and effective as Christians.

THIS LESSON AT A GLANCE

Section	Minutes	What Students Will Do	Supplies
Opener (Option 1)	5 to 10	**Quick Draw**—Draw childhood toys in a relay race.	Markers, 3×5 cards, newsprint, lollipops
(Option 2)		**Tricycle Race**—Participate in a guys vs. girls tricycle race.	Plastic cups, tricycles
Action and Reflection	10 to 15	**Who Are We Now?**—Examine a survey of kids' interests in a game show format.	Newsprint, markers
Bible Application	10 to 15	**Towers of Growth**—Explore what the Bible says about spiritual growth.	Bibles, shoe boxes, markers
Commitment	5 to 10	**Super Shield**—Create a coat of arms describing their lives.	"Super Shield" handouts (p. 19), pencils
Closing (Option 1)	5 to 10	**Growing Pins**—Use a childhood game to learn about trusting God.	Newsprint, marker, paper strips, tape, pencils, blindfolds, Bible
(Option 2)		**Away With Childish Things**—Choose childish characteristics they'll get rid of.	Bible, paper, pencils garbage bag

The Lesson

☐ OPTION 1: QUICK DRAW

Before kids arrive, write each toy from the "Toy List" in the margin on a separate 3×5 card. Separate the cards by category.

When everyone has arrived, ask:

● **What's your earliest childhood memory?**

Form two teams—guys on one and girls on the other. It's okay if the teams are uneven. Give each team newsprint and a marker. Tell teams they'll each guess common childhood toys as they're drawn by team members. Have the girls use the "Guys' Toys" cards, and have the guys use the "Girls' Toys" cards.

Have teams each choose one volunteer. Have volunteers each turn over the top card in their stack and draw the toy on their team's newsprint. The volunteer may not speak or write any words on the newsprint. When a team guesses the toy correctly, have another teammate draw the next word. The first team to guess all its words wins.

Declare a winner, and give kids each a lollipop for their efforts.

Then ask:

● **How easy was it to guess toys members of the opposite sex played with?** (Easy, I have a younger sister who plays with those toys; difficult, I never played with those toys.)

● **Do guys and girls play differently?** (No, each person has a unique personality regardless of sex; yes, they're born with built-in tendencies.)

● **What kind of toys did you play with—guys' or girls'?** (Guys', we never had any girl toys around; both, depending on whether I was playing with my brother or alone.)

● **Did you feel any pressure not to play with toys "inappropriate" for your sex? Explain.** (Yes, I wasn't supposed to play with dolls because they were only for girls; no, my parents wanted me to play with all kinds of toys.)

Say: **When you were very young, you probably didn't care whether you played with girls or guys. Then as you grew older, you may've found it more appropriate to play only in same-sex groups. But, as junior highers, you soon find that you want to know more about the opposite sex. This course will help you begin to understand guys and girls—and how to get along with each other.**

Toy List

"Guys' Toys"	"Girls' Toys"
● truck	● playhouse
● building blocks	● dolls
● electric train	● stuffed animals
● matchbox cars	● mother's clothes
● swing and slide	● jump rope
● coloring books	● coloring books

☐ OPTION 2: TRICYCLE RACE

This activity will require a smooth surface, such as a parking lot. Set up a simple circular race track using rocks or plastic cups to indicate the boundaries of the track.

Form two teams—girls on one and guys on the other. It's okay if teams are uneven. The number of people in the larger team determines the number of laps for the race.

Say: **We're going to have a guys vs. girls race using tricycles and the track indicated by the markers. Each person will ride the tricycle at least one lap around the track. In your team, line up alphabetically according to the first letters of your first names. If your team has fewer people than the other team, you'll need to have some people go to the end of the line after their turn and go around another lap during the race.**

Help the smaller team determine who'll take a second lap in the race. Then have the first person in each line sit on the tricycle (or stand behind it with one foot on the base, depending on the size of the tricycle). On "go," have kids peddle around the track. Once they reach the starting point, have the next person in line take his or her turn riding around the track. Remind kids to "drive safely" and avoid collisions.

If your group includes kids who're excessively overweight or handicapped, this activity may not work well with your group. You might use a variation of the race by having kids simply push a ball around the track with a broom.

When one team has its last person cross the finish line, call time and declare the winning team.

Ask:

● **Was this a fair race? Explain.** (Yes, each group had the same number of riders; no, the guys were faster.)

● **How is this race like the way guys and girls relate in everyday situations?** (We're always competing; we stick with members of our own sex.)

● **Why do guys and girls like to do things in same-sex groups?** (Guys are too gross to talk to; girls are always getting in the way; guys and girls like different things.)

Say: **As you've grown out of childhood, you've probably found most of your friends are of the same sex. It's easy to associate with only guys if you're a guy or only girls if you're a girl. But as you head into adulthood, you're going to want more friends of the opposite sex. This course will help you understand some of the differences and similarities guys and girls have—so you can get along better.**

WHO ARE WE NOW?

Form two teams with guys and girls in each team. Say: **We're going to play a guessing game about kids like you. One hundred middle school kids were surveyed about their lives. When I read the question, the first team will decide what number between one and 100 is the correct**

ACTION AND REFLECTION

(10 to 15 minutes)

answer. A majority of the team must agree on the answer before it's given. After an answer is given, the other team must guess whether the actual answer is higher or lower than the first team's answer. If the second team guesses right, it'll answer the next question first. If the second team guesses wrong, the first team will answer the next question first. Each question is worth 5,000 points. The final question is worth 20,000 points.

Flip a coin to determine which team goes first. Use the "Who Are We Now?" survey questions in the margin to start the game. Keep score on newsprint, and when the game is over declare a winner.

Form a circle and ask:

● **How'd you feel playing this game?** (Nervous; excited.)

● **Which did you like better: competing in the opener against a team of the opposite sex or competing in this game with mixed teams? Explain.** (I liked the opener, because we got to slaughter the guys in the race; I liked this game because teams were more even.)

● **What'd you like about this game?** (Getting the right answer; competing against the other team.)

● **What'd you dislike about the game?** (Not knowing the correct answers; trying to figure out what the kids in the survey thought.)

● **How is playing this game like growing up?** (You feel out of control, like you don't have any answers; you base your decisions on what other people think.)

Say: **In the game, the correct answers depended on the responses of kids like you. Likewise, as we grow into adulthood we often base our thoughts about what's "normal" on the opinions of those around us. If guys around you say girls are "gross," you might agree if you're a guy. Or if girls around you say some guy's "so immature," you might agree if you're a girl.**

● **Did the survey answers reflect your likes and interests? Explain.**

● **How are your present likes and interests the same as the likes and interests you had as a child?** (I'm still interested in cars, only now it's the real thing; I still talk to my dolls sometimes.)

● **How are your present likes and interests different from your childhood likes and interests?** (I'm interested in more "mature" things now, such as a career and sports; my interests have changed totally from when I was a child.)

Say: **When you compare the things that interested you as a child with the things that interest you now, you can**

Who Are We Now?

Use these survey questions to lead kids in playing the Who Are We Now? game.

1. Out of 100 girls surveyed, how many said their favorite Saturday activity was sleep? (62)

2. Out of 100 guys surveyed, how many said their favorite Saturday activity was sleep? (21)

3. Out of 100 girls surveyed, how many said the first thing they notice about a guy is his personality? (36)

4. Out of 100 guys surveyed, how many said the first thing they notice about a girl is her looks? (93)

5. Out of 100 kids (guys and girls) surveyed, how many said the best thing about growing up is more freedom? (39)

see how much you've changed. One thing that may not have changed much, though, is how you feel about the opposite sex. Some of you may want to ignore the opposite sex. But as you grow older, you'll need to learn to communicate with each other. We can learn how to do that by understanding how girls and guys each respond to issues of "growing up."

TOWERS OF GROWTH

Say: **The Bible doesn't mention puberty. It doesn't tell us how to deal with all the strange, new feelings you may be having. It does, however, share an incident from Christ's life when he was about your age.**

Have volunteers each read aloud one verse from Luke 2:41-52. After the reading, ask:

● **What was Jesus doing?** (Teaching the teachers; learning about God.)

● **How are you and Jesus similar in this passage?** (Like Jesus, I'm growing spiritually too; I don't see any similarities.)

● **What character traits does Jesus have that you want?** (He trusts God completely; he's confident of who he is.)

Form eight groups, and give each group a shoe box and a marker. (A group can be one person.) If you have fewer than eight people, form four groups and give each group two boxes. Have groups each read aloud 2 Peter 1:3-11. Assign groups each one of the "blocks" in the "tower of growth" from the passage: faith, goodness, knowledge, self-control, perseverance, godliness, brotherly kindness, and love. Define each of these terms for kids. Have groups each write on their block their quality and three ways kids might demonstrate this quality.

When groups are finished, have kids stack the blocks in the order they appear in the passage in the center of the room. Then have groups each explain their block.

Ask:

● **How is building this tower like "building" ourselves as we grow and mature?** (You have to realize each area of your life affects all the others; you have to be patient.)

● **How is this tower like the qualities it represents?** (As you grow in those qualities, you get higher so you can see more around you; the qualities are dependent on each other.)

● **Are there certain qualities girls or guys develop faster than the opposite sex? Explain.**

Have girls stack the blocks according to the importance they feel each item has—with the item they think is most important on top. Have the girls tell why they stacked the blocks in that order. Then have guys do the same. Discuss similarities guys and girls had in the order of items in their towers.

Say: **All the blocks work together to make us more like Christ. Although no one block is more important than another, the ultimate goal of all the blocks is love.**

Table Talk

The Table Talk activity in this course helps junior highers and middle schoolers discuss with their parents the differences between guys and girls as they grow up.

If you choose to use the Table Talk activity, this is a good time to show students the "Table Talk" handout (p. 20). Ask them to spend time with their parents completing it.

Before kids leave, give them each the "Table Talk" handout to take home, or tell them you'll be sending it to their parents.

Or use the Table Talk idea found in the Bonus Ideas (p. 45) for a meeting based on the handout.

SUPER SHIELD

Say: **Now let's see how these blocks might already be evident in your lives.**

Have kids spread out so no one is close together. Give kids each a "Super Shield" handout (p. 19) and a pencil. Say: **Complete the handout by drawing a picture for each section according to the instructions at the bottom of the page.**

When kids are finished, form pairs. As much as possible, have a guy and girl be partners. Have partners briefly share their completed handouts. Then have kids each say which tower of growth blocks are expressed in their partner's life. Refer to the tower for block names. Kids can mention more than one block for their partner.

Say: **As we can see from these Super Shields, both guys and girls have God-given strengths that'll help them grow and mature into adulthood. By recognizing each other's strengths, we can learn to respect each other for who we are, not what sex we happen to be.**

Have kids each silently commit to looking for positive qualities in others, regardless of their gender.

☐ OPTION 1: GROWING PINS

Say: **As we grow up, we grow out of certain childhood activities. But we can still learn from the games we played as kids. Today we're going to end the lesson with a variation on a familiar party game, Pin the Tail on the Donkey.**

Form no fewer than three teams. Have each team pick a representative to play Pin the Tail on the Donkey. Draw a stick-figure donkey onto a sheet of newsprint. Give representatives each a paper strip with tape at one end. Have them each write their name on it. Have teams cheer for their representative, but don't allow them to give directions.

Blindfold each representative. One at a time, spin the representatives and have them stick their tails as close to the target as possible. Don't allow representatives to remove their

COMMITMENT

(5 to 10 minutes)

CLOSING

(5 to 10 minutes)

blindfolds until the game is over. After the last representative is finished, have representatives each remove their blindfold. Ask the representatives:

● **What did you think about this game?** (It was fun; I'd forgotten how hard it was.)

● **How do some kids approach the opposite sex as if they were wearing blindfolds?** (Some kids don't have a clue what girls or guys are like; some kids don't know how to talk to members of the opposite sex; some people only look at how others look, not who they are.)

● **What can we do to "take off the blindfolds" as we deal with members of the opposite sex?** (Learn what they like to do; talk with them; try to understand who they are as people.)

Say: **Even if you feel awkward, clumsy or self-conscious around girls or guys, you can trust God because he knows what you're going through.**

Read aloud 2 Corinthians 5:17. Close with a prayer asking for God's help for girls and guys to grow spiritually as well as emotionally and physically.

☐ OPTION 2: AWAY WITH CHILDISH THINGS

Say: **As we grow up and learn to relate to the opposite sex, we need to put away childish attitudes and actions. Then we can spend quality time getting to know each other as people—no matter what sex we are.**

Read aloud 1 Corinthians 13:11-12. Give kids each a sheet of paper and a pencil. Have kids each write on their paper one childish characteristic they'll get rid of. For example, kids might write, "temper tantrums" or "fighting." When kids are finished, go around the circle holding out a garbage bag. As you walk by, have kids each read aloud their childish trait, then crumple the paper and throw it in the bag. Form a circle and close in prayer. Thank God for helping kids grow spiritually, emotionally and physically.

If You Still Have Time . . .

Are They for Real?—Form groups of no more than five. Give each group paper and a pencil. Have group members list movies or TV shows about older teenagers. Have groups list the dominate qualities of the teenage characters, then divide the characters according to whether group members think the characters are "real" or "Hollywood." Have groups share their lists with each other. Then have kids tell what older teenage qualities they want to develop.

Girls and Guys—Write the words "girls and guys" vertically down the middle of a sheet of newsprint or on a chalkboard. Have kids work together to brainstorm words or phrases illustrating positive aspects of both girls and guys, using the letters to form an acrostic. For example:

Good Listeners	**A**lways kind	**G**enerous
Interested in relationships	**N**ice to others	**U**nderstanding
Ready to help	**D**ependable	**Y**oung at heart
Likable		**S**mart
Super friends		

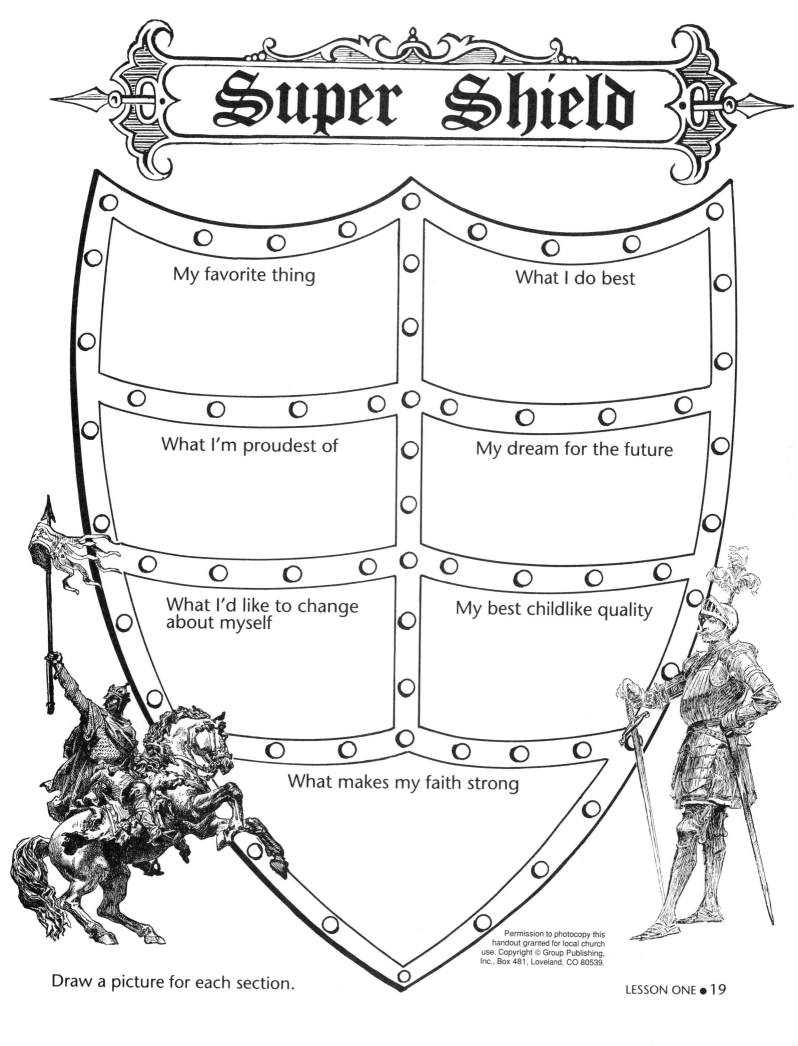

Super Shield

My favorite thing

What I do best

What I'm proudest of

My dream for the future

What I'd like to change about myself

My best childlike quality

What makes my faith strong

Draw a picture for each section.

Table Talk

To the Parent: We're involved in a junior high course at church called *Guys & Girls: Understanding Each Other*. Students are exploring a Christian perspective on puberty and relationships between guys and girls. We'd like you and your teenager to spend some time discussing these important topics. Use this page to help you do that.

Parent
- What was your biggest frustration during puberty?
- Were you an early or a late bloomer? How did that affect your self-image?
- What's the most exciting change you see in your junior higher right now?
- What change in your junior higher are you having the most trouble with? Explain.
- What do you need from your child in the next few years?

Junior higher
- What part of puberty are you the most unsure of or afraid of?
- What do you like best about your body right now? least?
- What questions do you have about sexuality?
- What do you admire most about your parents?
- In what ways do you want to grow up to be like them?
- What do you need from your parents right now?

Parent and junior higher
Growing up
- What's your favorite childhood memory?
- What was your favorite childhood toy?
- What childlike qualities do you still have today?
- What was your relationship with Jesus like when you were a child?
- What's it like now?
- In what way have you changed most since you were a child?

Male and female roles
- What's your idea of the "perfect woman"?
- What's your idea of the "perfect man"?
- Why do men and women make such good partners for each other?

Read Mark 4:35-41 together. Tell two ways you'll try to calm the storms of family life that come during the puberty years.

GUYS & *Girls:*
UNDERSTANDING EACH OTHER

BODY DIFFERENCES

Joe hates the locker room. He's not as "hairy" as the other guys and he feels humiliated by their stares. Joe wonders: Am I normal?

All the girls envy Susan. She's the first girl to wear a bra. The boys constantly tease her. But Susan desperately wishes she just looked like everyone else.

Junior highers' bodies often betray them. During puberty, physical development is rapid and confusing. Understanding these changes offsets the self-esteem plunge that often strikes kids down during this time.

LESSON AIM

To help junior highers understand and cope with the physical changes of puberty.

OBJECTIVES

Students will:
- **understand the changes they experience as they move through puberty;**
- **learn to view their bodies through God's eyes;**
- **utilize scripture to cope with puberty;**
- **discover how guys and girls deal with physical changes in puberty; and**
- **recognize their positive qualities and physical assets.**

BIBLE BASIS

GENESIS 1:26-31
PSALM 139:13-16
SONG OF SONGS 4:1-7; 5:10-16

Look up the following scriptures. Then read the background paragraphs to see how the passages relate to your junior highers and middle schoolers.

In **Genesis 1:26-31**, God creates man and woman.

Man and woman are created in God's image. God called us good. He was pleased with his creation.

Junior highers need to understand that they're made in God's image. When they put themselves down because of their looks, they pass judgment on God's handiwork. Knowing God used himself as a model when he made people—both men and women—will boost kids' self-esteem and help them endure puberty.

In **Psalm 139:13-16**, the Psalmist is in awe of God's handiwork in creating him.

The Psalmist is amazed at the intricate workings of the body. We're each designed personally by God. He knows who we'll be and what we'll look like before we're even born.

Junior highers often dislike their bodies. This passage can reassure them how beautiful they are to God. He's planned each person for his glory. Kids' bodies are his wonderful works, even in the process of puberty.

In **Song of Songs 4:1-7; 5:10-16**, the writer expounds the beauty of the human body.

These passages contain poems that highlight and praise the human body. In chapter 4, the man describes the woman he loves. And the male physique is praised in chapter 5.

Even though they may be unsure of the changes happening to their bodies, junior highers should be encouraged from these verses. Their bodies are like beautiful, unfolding blossoms. In God's love, we're all seen as magnificently as the lovers see each other in Song of Songs.

THIS LESSON AT A GLANCE

Section	Minutes	What Students Will Do	Supplies
Opener (Option 1)	5 to 10	**Clumps of Clay**—Make clay creations to simulate early and late bloomers.	Wax paper, modeling clay or Play-Doh
(Option 2)		**World's Best**—Vote on the world's best-looking man and woman.	Newsprint, markers,
Action and Reflection	10 to 15	**What's New?**—Learn physical changes that happen during puberty.	Newsprint, markers, Bibles
Bible Application	10 to 15	**Pits and Zits**—Use scripture to answer a "Dear Hunk" letter.	"Dear Hunk" handouts (p. 29), pencils, Bibles,
Commitment	10 to 15	**We're Okay**—Describe positive things about each other and commit to being sensitive to each other's concerns about physical changes.	Paper, pencils, tape
Closing (Option 1)	up to 5	**Under Construction**—Create posters to remind them they're still under construction.	Construction paper, markers
(Option 2)		**Personal Poems**—Create poems that describe how unique they are.	3×5 cards, pencils

Note: This lesson deals with a sensitive issue—junior highers and their bodies. You may find this to be a difficult lesson, but it's worth it. Kids will likely leave this lesson with a better understanding of the opposite sex—and a realization that they're not alone as they deal with physical changes of puberty.

The Lesson

☐ OPTION 1: CLUMPS OF CLAY

Give kids each a piece of wax paper and a lump of modeling clay or Play-Doh. Tell kids to decide what they'll sculpt out of the clay but not to tell anyone what they plan to make. Allow kids to start sculpting their clay. After a few minutes, have kids try to guess what others are making. Tell kids not to reveal what they're making if no one guesses. Point out that some objects are almost finished, while others are barely started.

Have kids each continue their sculpting. After a few more minutes, have kids try again to guess what others are making. Emphasize the various stages of completion.

Ask:

● **Why didn't everyone complete his or her sculpture?** (There wasn't enough time; some sculptures were more complicated.)

● **Was the first sculpture finished necessarily the best one?** (No, getting finished first has nothing to do with how good it is; yes, all the rest of the sculptures are incomplete.)

● Say: **Your clay sculptures are like guys' and girls' physical development during puberty. Just as the sculptures were at various stages of completion, people develop at different rates. You each designed and planned your sculpture. God also has a design and plan for your physical growth.**

☐ OPTION 2: WORLD'S BEST

On newsprint, have kids each list their nomination for the nation's best-looking man and woman. When the nominations are over, hold an election to determine kids' choice for the best-looking man and woman.

Ask:

● **What makes the winners good-looking?** (Physically fit bodies; beautiful eyes.)

● Say: **I want you to think about how you feel about your own body. Spend a moment in silent reflection about how you feel.**

Be sensitive to kids who are fat, skinny, pimple-faced and so on. Some kids will have a difficult time with this reflection time.

● **Is the way a person looks really what matters in life? Explain.** (No, what matters is the kind of person you are; yes, because people judge you on how you look.)

● **Why are we tempted to compare the way we look with others?** (Because we want to fit in; because we want to know we're normal.)

Say: **You don't need to worry about whether you'll grow up to look like the best-looking man or woman. You'll be uniquely handsome or beautiful. But getting there can be frustrating—especially because of all the changes that come during puberty.**

Table Talk Follow-Up

If you sent the "Table Talk" handout (p. 20) to parents last week, discuss students' reactions to the activity. Ask volunteers to share what they learned from the discussion with their parents.

ACTION AND REFLECTION
(10 to 15 minutes)

WHAT'S NEW?

Say: **Let's look at the changes our bodies go through during puberty.**

Form two groups—guys in one group, girls in the other. It's okay if the two groups are uneven. Give each group newsprint and markers. Have groups each list all the physical changes that take place in the opposite sex during puberty.

This may be an uncomfortable assignment for some junior highers, but they can work through it with encouragement and guidance. Let them know you think they can handle it with maturity. Still, expect some giggling and secretiveness.

After a few minutes, have groups share their lists with the whole group.

Use the "Beautiful Bodies" summary on page 25 to correct any misinformation or add new information to the groups' lists.

Ask girls:

● **What surprised you about what the guys listed as girls' changes?** (They got a lot of the changes right; they listed some strange things.)

Ask guys:

● **What surprised you about what the girls listed as guys' changes?** (They didn't know what to list; they listed a lot of things that are true.)

Ask everyone:

● **How'd you feel as you made the lists and told about them?** (Embarrassed; nervous.)

● **What made this activity uncomfortable?** (I don't know

anything about this topic; I wondered what other people would think of my answers.)

● **How is this uncomfortable feeling like the way we feel about the changes in guys' and girls' bodies?** (I wonder what other people think of me; I feel awkward because I don't know much about what's happening to my body.)

Say: **Talking about our bodies is sometimes embarrassing. But in Song of Songs, King Solomon praises the human body. He saw no shame in the beauty of our bodies, which are created by God.**

Have the guys silently read Song of Songs 4:1-7. Have the girls silently read Song of Songs 5:10-16. Expect some giggles—kids will probably feel uncomfortable reading these passages.

After kids finish reading their scripture, have them form a circle. Say: **How did these passages make you feel? Make a facial expression to indicate how the passage made you feel. You may've been surprised, upset or confused. Hold your facial expression for a minute and look around at the other kids' expressions.**

Ask:

● **How are the responses kids had to the scripture similar and different?** (Many were confused or upset; some were indifferent and some were bothered or embarrassed.)

Have guys and girls summarize the passages they read. Song of Songs 4:1-7 is a description of a beautiful woman. Song of Songs 5:10-16 is a description of a handsome man.

Ask:

● **What are similar responses guys and girls have to the physical changes they're going through in puberty?** (Both are nervous; both don't understand what's happening; both are self-conscious.)

● **What were you thinking as you read your Song of Songs scripture?** (I couldn't believe anything like this was in the Bible; I was embarrassed.)

● **What's the difference between these passages and the way the media portrays the human body?** (Television and movies portray people as objects, but the Bible emphasizes love; the people in the Bible communicate more than people in movies.)

● **What can we learn about our bodies from these scriptures?** (God thinks my body is okay; I'm beautiful in God's eyes.)

● **What can we learn about our feelings toward the opposite sex from these scriptures?** (It's okay to feel attracted to girls; I don't have to be embarrassed about the way I feel.)

● **How have your feelings about the opposite sex**

Beautiful Bodies

Use this information to correct or supplement kids' ideas about changes that happen during puberty.

Male Changes
● Grow to full height
● Body hair grows
● Skin gets oilier (acne may strike!)
● Reproductive organs grow
● Voice deepens
● Whiskers start to grow
● Rapid shift in emotions
● Sexual desires increase

Female Changes
● Grow to full height
● Body hair grows
● Skin gets oilier (acne may attack!)
● Breasts grow
● Menstruation begins
● Sexual desires increase
● Rapid shift in emotions

changed in the past year or two? (I really like being around girls now; I want guys to notice me now.)

Say: **Our sexuality is part of God's plan for us. But puberty can be a difficult step on the road to maturity because of all the "pits" and "zits" we encounter.**

PITS AND ZITS

Form groups of no more than four, this time mixing guys and girls. Give groups each a "Dear Hunk" handout (p. 29) and a pencil. Have groups each read the letters on the handouts, then have them each read Genesis 1:26-31 and Psalm 139:13-16. Tell groups to each answer the letters using the scripture as the basis for their response. Have them each write their responses on the back of the handout.

Be sensitive to group members who may feel like the people described on the handout. If you've got kids who have lots of acne or are obviously "late bloomers," be prepared; kids might tease them during this activity. Some kids might even put themselves down because of similar feelings of low self-esteem. Use this time to talk about how guys and girls deal with physical changes that make them feel less than perfect.

If someone does put down another group member, don't draw attention to the putdown. Simply move on with the lesson. It's likely that person also feels self-conscious and responds to that by teasing others.

If a student is way out of line, quietly take him or her aside and agree on a time to talk after class.

When groups are finished, have them read aloud the "Dear Hunk" letters and their replies.

Then ask:

● **Have you ever felt like the guy or girl in these letters? How'd you handle it?** (Yes, I rejected those people who rejected me; I found new friends.)

● **How can these scriptures help us work through those bad situations?** (I can remember that God still accepts me; I can forgive others because God loves them too.)

● **How'd the scriptures help you answer the letters?** (They pointed out the truth that God accepts us and loves us; they helped us see a different perspective on our bodies.)

● **How do these scriptures relate to the physical changes that occur during puberty?** (When we feel bad about the way we look, we can remember that God is in control; we can see puberty as God molding us into men and women.)

● **What can you learn from this activity about the changes going on in the opposite sex?** (Guys and girls both have lots of changes; guys and girls feel self-conscious about physical things.)

Say: **While your bodies are changing and developing, it's normal to feel weird sometimes. One way to get out of the pits is to recognize you're special. No matter what** you're going through, God loves you and you can be proud of who you are right now.

WE'RE OKAY

Give kids each a sheet of paper and a pencil. Have kids each write one or two words on their paper that describe how the physical changes of puberty make them feel. Kids may write negative words such as angry, embarrassed or scared. Or kids may write positive words such as hopeful, pleased or encouraged.

Say: **As you go through the many physical changes of puberty, you may feel less than great about yourself—or you may feel pretty good. Either way, we can always feel better about ourselves when others encourage us or give us compliments.**

Have kids each tape their paper on their back, with the feeling words facing out.

Say: **On "go," write on another person's paper one thing you appreciate about that person's personality, faith or physical appearance. Say only positive things and avoid crude comments about physical appearance. Things such as "You're always kind," "Your love for God really shows" or "You have pretty eyes" are fine. Write your comments on the flip side of the feeling words. Do this for more than four people—at least one guy and one girl.**

Make sure everyone has at least one person write positive things about him or her. If possible, go around to each person yourself and write something positive. Then form a circle. Have kids each hold their papers in front of them, with the feeling words facing out.

Say: **The feelings represented on these papers may be as different as the people holding them. But while guys and girls have different reactions to the physical changes they're dealing with, a pat on the back can help make each person feel good about who he or she is.**

Have kids simultaneously flip their papers so they can each read the positive comments written on their paper.

Ask:

● **How do these positive comments make you feel?** (Happy; encouraged; loved.)

● **How can supporting each other in the difficult time of puberty help you better survive growing up?** (We see how we're all in this together; we share concerns and joys; we boost each other's self-esteem.)

● **You've seen how puberty affects guys and girls in a substantial way. How can that understanding positively affect how you deal with the opposite sex?** (I can be more caring; I'll stop teasing girls or guys about certain things; I'll know better what to say and what not to say.)

Form two groups—guys in one group, girls in the other. (A group can be one person.) Have groups each come up with

COMMITMENT
(10 to 15 minutes)

two practical things they'll do to show their respect for the physical changes members of the opposite sex are going through. For example, guys might say, "We'll stop making rude comments to girls about their figures." Girls might say, "We'll stop making negative comments about guys' heights."

Ask kids each to make a commitment to being sensitive to physical changes guys and girls are going through in puberty.

CLOSING
(up to 5 minutes)

☐ OPTION 1: UNDER CONSTRUCTION

Give kids each a sheet of construction paper and a marker. Say: **Puberty is a time of great change for guys and girls. Sometimes the change comes rapidly; sometimes it seems much too slow. But even as we grow into adults, God is continually helping us become the best we can be.**

Have kids each create a poster describing how they're still under construction as junior highers. Encourage kids to include on their posters positive words of encouragement, such as "Hang in there, God isn't finished with you yet" or "Growing up isn't easy, but God is with you every step of the way."

Have kids each display their poster for the rest of the class. Close with prayer, thanking God for the gift of puberty.

☐ OPTION 2: PERSONAL POEMS

Give kids each a 3×5 card and a pencil. Have kids each write a poem describing their own body and feelings. The poem should follow this format:

1st line: (junior higher's first name)
2nd line: (two action words describing the junior higher)
3rd line: (three physical characteristics the junior higher possesses)
4th line: (four emotions the junior higher feels)
5th line: (five interests the junior higher has)
6th line: (Write and complete the sentence: "Thanks, God, for making me . . . ")
7th line: (junior higher's first name)

Use this example to help kids get started:

Linda
Reads, jogs
Blue eyes, curly hair, little feet
Happy, excited, curious, tired
Puppets, guitar, softball, writing, sleep
Thanks, God, for making me caring
Linda

When everyone is finished, have kids each read aloud their poem. Praise kids' efforts. Then close with prayer, thanking God for making us all masterpieces in his eyes.

If You Still Have Time . . .

Super Survey—Have kids visit an adult Sunday school class during the lesson for an impromptu survey. Have kids ask adults each to think back to their junior high years and say the first word that comes to mind when kids say each of the words or phrases from the list below. Have kids each say the words or phrases one at a time and record adults' responses.

Here's the list:
- puberty
- the opposite sex
- growing up

Have kids return to the room and discuss the similarities and differences between adults' responses and the way kids feel today.

God's Bod Meditation—Have kids stand or sit on the floor in a circle. Have them each turn toward the person on their right and begin to give him or her a back rub.

Say: **I'm going to read a message from God to you based on Psalm 139:13-16. As I read, close your eyes, enjoy the back rub and let God speak to you.**

Read aloud this message: **I created your innermost being. I knit you together in your mother's womb. You're fearfully and wonderfully made, for my work is always wonderful. Your body wasn't hidden from me when I made you before you were born. I know where each of your muscles connects. I crafted your skeleton. I caused your heart to beat. I know the number of hairs on your head. I crafted your fingerprint. I created you in my image for my glory. I will be with you always for I love you.**

After a few minutes of silence, ask kids how the message affected their perspective on themselves and others.

Dear Hunk

Read the letters and respond using Genesis 1:26-31 and Psalm 139:13-16 as your basis.

Dear Hunk,

I hate myself. I used to be the best-looking guy in my class. Now I'm a mess. I trip over my big feet, sweat like a pig and my face is full of zits. All the girls call me "Crater Face." No one will come near me, and I don't have friends anymore. I feel ugly and all alone. What should I do?

Signed,
Full of Zits

Dear Hunk,

I've got an awful problem. All the other girls in my class have gotten their periods already. I haven't even started to get breasts. I think maybe something's wrong with me. It's even worse in front of the boys. They all call me the "Ironed Maiden," because I'm flat as a board. What should I do?

Signed,
In the Pits

BATTLE OF THE SEXES

Macho men and frivolous females. Our society often encourages unhealthy stereotypes. Male and female sex roles are constantly battled in today's war between the sexes. Understanding and appreciating the opposite sex has become an important issue for kids going through puberty.

LESSON AIM

To help junior highers put sex roles and stereotypes in a Christian perspective.

OBJECTIVES

Students will:
● identify positive characteristics of each sex;
● examine what the Bible says about relationships between men and women;
● experience a "battle of the sexes"; and
● brainstorm positive ways to fill their minds with godly views of the opposite sex.

BIBLE BASIS

GENESIS 2:18-25
GALATIANS 3:26—4:7

Look up the following scriptures. Then read the background paragraphs to see how the passages relate to your junior highers and middle schoolers.

In **Genesis 2:18-25**, God creates woman from the rib of man.

God knows it's not good for man to be alone. For Adam to realize the depth of his human potential, he needed a suitable helper.

In the junior higher's world, masculine and feminine roles are in conflict. Kids need to know that God made men and women to complement each other—not to compete.

In **Galatians 3:26—4:7**, Paul says faith in Christ makes us all sons of God and heirs to the kingdom.

Unity in Christ knocks down the walls between the sexes and stereotypes. We're no longer only servants. Faith makes us full heirs of God.

As kids go through puberty, everything around them seems to be changing. Kids need to know that God is their one constant in life. His promises can guide kids through the maze of sexual roles and stereotypes.

THIS LESSON AT A GLANCE

Section	Minutes	What Students Will Do	Supplies
Opener (Option 1)	up to 5	**Marching Madness**—Role play conformity and march to the same tune.	"Marching Methods" cards (p. 36), toy drum or something similar
(Option 2)		**Pink and Blue Thoughts**—List positive characteristics of being male or female.	Newsprint, markers
Action and Reflection	15 to 20	**Battle of the Sexes**—Express how they feel about sexual stereotypes.	Magazines, construction paper, scissors
Bible Application	10 to 15	**Break the Mold**—List what makes men and women good for each other.	Bibles, newsprint, pencils
Commitment	5 to 10	**Mind Boggles**—Brainstorm positive ways to fill your mind.	Newsprint, markers
Closing (Option 1)	5 to 10	**Gingerbread Prayer**—Thank God for creating man and woman.	Gingerbread men or women cookies
(Option 2)		**Discoveries**—Share things they've learned from this lesson.	3×5 cards, pencils

The Lesson

☐ OPTION 1: MARCHING MADNESS

Have kids form a circle with you in the middle. Tell kids they'll be playing the role of musicians hoping to be selected as new marching band members. Give kids each a different "Marching Methods" card (p. 36). On "go," have kids each begin to march around in a circle using the marching method described on their card. Don't allow kids to speak. Use a toy drum or something similar to establish a marching beat.

OPENER
(up to 5 minutes)

After 30 seconds, say: **You look silly! Don't you know how to march? Get your act together or you're out of the band!**

Wait another 30 seconds and observe. If the "offbeat" marchers begin to conform to others' standard march, praise them. After 30 seconds, reprimand the marchers again. Make your comments directly to the kids who are still marching differently from the others.

Wait another 30 seconds, then stop the marchers and ask:

● **How'd you feel marching around in a circle?** (Stupid; okay until you started scolding us.)

● **What happened after I corrected you the first time?** (Some people changed the way they marched; I started taking it more seriously.)

● **How does this activity illustrate conformity?** (People started out different but ended up the same; everyone was pressured to march alike.)

Say: **Although society is constantly changing, it still pressures guys and girls to act in certain ways. Guys are encouraged not to let their feelings show too much. They're taught to handle every situation with strength and a logical attitude. Girls are cautioned not to be too assertive or sure of themselves. They're encouraged to let guys take the lead in most situations. Today we'll compare God's view of guys and girls with society's.**

☐ OPTION 2: PINK AND BLUE THOUGHTS

Form two groups—guys in one, girls in the other. It's okay if the groups are uneven. Give each group newsprint and markers.

Say: **Girls and guys argue over which is the better sex. Today you have a chance to prove once and for all that your sex is better.**

On "go," have girls list what they like best about being female, and have guys list what they like best about being male. Tell kids the group with the longest list after two minutes is the winner.

After the contest, have groups each explain their list. Declare the group with the longest list the winner. Encourage the winners to celebrate.

Tempers may run high in this activity. Don't do anything to settle kids down at this point. Sexual biases will make the next activity even more effective.

BATTLE OF THE SEXES

Designate one side of the room as "Guys' Activities" and the other side as "Girls' Activities." Read the activities one at a time from the "Guys vs. Girls" box on page 33. Have kids each stand on one side of the room or the other, depending on whether they think an activity is more male-oriented or female-oriented.

ACTION AND REFLECTION

(15 to 20 minutes)

Kids must stand at one wall or the other—no middle ground. After kids choose sides for each activity, have volunteers explain why they chose as they did.

After the activity, ask:

● **Did the guys and girls line up differently? Why or why not?** (No, because everyone knows what's expected of them; yes, because the girls thought they could do everything.)

● **How does our society tell us what is "male" and "female"?** (Through television and movies; through famous people who act as role models.)

● **How do you feel if you have a personality trait or like to do a job that's considered part of the opposite sex's role?** (I don't let anyone know; I feel adventurous, like I'm breaking out of a mold.)

Give kids each a magazine. Have kids each tear out any full-page picture, but don't allow kids to show anyone their picture. Give kids each a sheet of construction paper. Provide scissors for kids to share.

Say: **In a moment, cut out a 2-inch "window" in your construction paper. Then cover your magazine picture with the construction paper. Let others view only the part of your picture that the window reveals. The goal is to keep others from guessing what your picture is, so choose carefully where you'll cut your window.**

Have kids each cut out their window and cover their picture. Form groups of six or fewer. Have kids each show their covered picture to their group. Have groups try to guess what each person's picture is. Give 1 point to the first person who guesses correctly for each picture.

After all the pictures have been guessed, call everyone together.

Then ask:

● **How'd you feel trying to guess what the pictures were?** (Confused; frustrated because I couldn't figure out what it was.)

● **What made it so hard to guess what the picture was?** (Most of it was covered up; I only got to see an unimportant part.)

● **How is trying to guess the pictures' identities like trying to understand relationships between guys and girls?** (We only understand a little about guys and girls right now; we'll learn more about relationships as we grow older.)

● **What might the construction paper represent?** (Lack of experience; stereotypes.)

● **How can you expand your understanding of the opposite sex?** (Ask God to teach me; get to know more girls as friends.)

Say: **It's normal to feel frustrated at not understanding**

Guys vs. Girls

- watching television
- decorating the home
- being unemotional
- mowing the yard
- taking care of children
- crying
- cleaning house
- cooking meals
- playing sports
- feeling romantic
- paying for a date
- being moody
- shopping for groceries
- being realistic

something that's different from what we know—like the opposite sex. And there are many ways to learn more about guys and girls. One of the best ways is through the Bible. God's Word gives us clues about the relationship God wants between men and women. Let's look at what the Bible says about stereotypes and sex roles.

BIBLE APPLICATION
(10 to 15 minutes)

BREAK THE MOLD

Have kids return to their same-sex groups. Give groups each a Bible, a sheet of newsprint and several pencils. Have girls draw a gingerbread man on their newsprint. Have the guys draw a gingerbread woman. Have groups each read aloud Genesis 2:18-25. Then have groups each list inside their gingerbread person all the qualities that make the opposite sex suitable for them. For example, kids might list willingness to talk openly, sense of humor or caring attitude. When groups are finished, have them each explain their list.

Then form a circle and ask:

● **What are some specific qualities you want in a boyfriend or girlfriend?**

Say: **Each of us has many positive qualities to offer a potential boyfriend or girlfriend. Let's name a few for each person.**

Have kids each say two positive qualities about the person on their right that would make him or her a neat girlfriend or boyfriend. For example, someone might say, "You have a neat sense of humor" or "You're really fun to talk to." If someone has trouble thinking of something to say, have others in the group offer suggestions.

Say: **As you get to know the opposite sex, lots of thoughts fill your mind. It's easy to concentrate on all the ways you seem to fall short of your expectations. But the Bible shows us how to handle the pressures of puberty and relationships with the opposite sex.**

COMMITMENT
(5 to 10 minutes)

MIND BOGGLES

Read aloud Philippians 4:8-9. Say: **When you feel awkward about your abilities to relate to the opposite sex, the Bible says you should fill your minds with true, noble, right, pure, lovely, admirable, excellent and praiseworthy thoughts about yourself and your relationships. Then God's peace will strengthen you.**

Have kids sit in a circle. Lay a sheet of newsprint on the floor in the center of the circle, and give kids each a marker. Have junior highers each write on the newsprint one idea for filling their mind with godly thoughts. If needed, offer suggestions such as read the Bible daily, listen to my parents or take notes on the sermon. After kids each have written one suggestion, go around the circle again and have kids each write a second suggestion.

Form pairs. Have partners each choose one idea from the newsprint they'll focus on this week. Encourage partners to check up on each other sometime this week.

☐ OPTION 1: GINGERBREAD PRAYER

Have kids stand in a circle. Give kids each a gingerbread man or woman. Explain that unlike these cookies, which all look the same, God has created each young teenager with a special uniqueness—a uniqueness that suits them perfectly to relate to the opposite sex.

Allow kids to eat their cookies. Have kids close with prayer, praising God for our differences and thanking him for creating the beautiful combination of man and woman.

☐ OPTION 2: DISCOVERIES

Give kids each a 3×5 card and a pencil. Have them each write three things they've learned from this lesson. When kids are finished, form groups of four or fewer and have kids each tell what they wrote. When groups are finished, call everyone together and have volunteers repeat what they shared in their group.

Close with prayer, thanking God for creating two different sexes to complement each other.

CLOSING
(5 to 10 minutes)

If You Still Have Time . . .

Why Are You?—Form two groups—guys in one and girls in the other. Give groups each paper and a pencil. Have groups each brainstorm three questions they still have about the opposite sex. When groups are ready, have them each read their questions to the other group. Allow girls to respond to guys' questions. Then allow guys to respond to girls' questions.

The Great Debate—Have a girls vs. guys debate on the roles men and women should have in society. Have kids debate the following questions:
- Should men and women be expected to do all things equally?
- Are there any jobs appropriate only for men? women?

Encourage positive discussion about the issue of equality. Use Galatians 3:28 and 1 Timothy 2:11-13 to spark discussion on these issues.

MARCHING METHODS

Photocopy and cut apart these cards. Give one card to each junior higher. It's okay if most kids have the "regular step" card.

March backward.

March by skipping.

March with your left knee higher than your right knee.

March by jumping.

March for three beats and then twirl around.

Take huge marching steps.

Take tiny marching steps.

March forward with one regular step.

March forward with one regular step.

March forward with one regular step.

March forward with one regular step.

March forward with one regular step.

UPS AND DOWNS

Junior highers and middle schoolers live on an emotional roller coaster. While junior high girls may cry at TV commercials, junior high guys try to look tough—even when they feel like crying. Guys and girls go through many different emotions as they grow into adulthood. By understanding the differences in guys' and girls' emotional development, guys and girls can better communicate and relate to one another.

To help junior highers understand the similarities and differences in guys' and girls' emotions.

LESSON AIM

Students will:
- **discover how guys and girls may show feelings in different ways;**
- **become aware of the range of their feelings and accept that fluctuating feelings are a normal part of puberty;**
- **explore how biblical characters dealt with fear and apprehension;**
- **understand how events and situations may influence feelings and emotions; and**
- **identify positive ways of managing negative feelings.**

OBJECTIVES

Look up the following scriptures. Then read the background paragraphs to see how the passages relate to your junior highers and middle schoolers.

In **Joshua 1:1-11**, God charges Joshua to be Moses' successor and lead Israel into the Promised Land.

God's message to Joshua: To be successful, obey God's law. Knowing Joshua's anxiety, God encourages him by saying God will be with him wherever he goes.

Junior highers can learn two lessons from this passage. God will be with them as they begin to take on the attributes of adulthood. Their success will be gauged by how well they

BIBLE BASIS
JOSHUA 1:1-11
MARK 4:35-41

follow God's law. Kids can take comfort in this passage as they enter the insecurities of puberty.

In **Mark 4:35-41**, Jesus calms the sea.

Sudden storms were prevalent on the Sea of Galilee. When Jesus stilled the water, he made it clear to his disciples that he is Lord over all creation.

It's spectacular to think that Jesus could calm a storm with a word. But for junior highers, the symbolic meaning is just as awesome. In the turbulence of puberty, Jesus can calm the storms of fear, sorrow, confusion and changes for those who place their faith in him.

THIS LESSON AT A GLANCE

Section	Minutes	What Students Will Do	Supplies
Opener (Option 1) (Option 2)	5 to 10	**Name That Feeling**—List feeling words. **Emotion Statues**—Sculpt a human-emotion statue.	Paper, markers, newsprint
Action and Reflection	10 to 15	**The Terrible, Horrible, Super, Wonderful Day**—Listen to a story and respond to it based on how they feel.	
Bible Application	10 to 15	**Who's Afraid of the Big Bad Wolf?**—Act out a Bible story and discuss feelings of fear and apprehension.	Bibles, paper, pencils
Commitment	10 to 15	**Emotion Potions**—Complete a handout about personal feelings.	"Emotion Potion" handouts (p. 44), pencils, pitcher, water, baking pan, glass
Closing (Option 1) (Option 2)	up to 5	**How I Feel**—Creatively express how they feel about emotions expressed by the opposite sex. **Happy (and Sad) Together**—Act out different feelings together.	Construction paper

The Lesson

☐ OPTION 1: NAME THAT FEELING

Form two teams—guys vs. girls. It's okay if the teams are uneven. Give each team paper and a marker. Have teams write down as many "feelings" words as possible; for example: love, hate, fear, and joy. The more words groups think of, the better chance they have of winning.

After two minutes, have teams each sit in separate circles. Take turns asking each team to share a feeling word. List words on newsprint. Alternate until one team has run out of words. Words may not be used more than once. The last team to share a feeling word wins.

After the activity, ask:

● **What were the differences between girls' answers and guys' answers?** (Girls named more romantic feelings; guys named more strong, macho feelings.)

● **What are the most common feelings of kids your age?** (Fear; embarrassment; anger; silliness; depression.)

Say: **There are a lot of feeling words for the huge variety of emotions people have. We can only understand ourselves when we can identify how we're feeling. Today we're going to examine our feelings and how guys' and girls' feelings are different and similar.**

☐ OPTION 2: EMOTION STATUES

Form same-sex pairs. Have partners each think of four emotions they've felt today. Assign one person in each pair to be "Romeo" and the other to be "Juliet." Have Romeo whisper one of his or her emotions to Juliet. Then have Juliet "sculpt" Romeo like a mannequin to convey that emotion. After Juliets each have sculpted their Romeo, have Romeos hold their poses while Juliets walk through the gallery of emotions. Have kids try to guess the emotions portrayed.

Repeat the process, this time letting the Romeos sculpt the Juliets. After the second art "tour," have everyone sit down.

Ask:

● **How are these sculptures like our emotions?** (They were easy to change; they were out for everybody to see.)

● **What'd this activity tell you about your feelings?** (They're easy to mix up with the wrong body language; they change a lot in a day.)

● **How do feelings guys and girls have differ?** (Girls cry more; guys try to always act tough; guys don't share their feelings much.)

Say: **It's important to identify your feelings, so you can be able to understand yourself and others better. We may** think only girls cry or only guys try to act tough, but our emotions are much deeper than that. Today we'll take a look at how guys' and girls' emotions differ and how they're the same.

ACTION AND REFLECTION
(10 to 15 minutes)

THE TERRIBLE, HORRIBLE, SUPER, WONDERFUL DAY

Have kids sit in a circle.

Say: **During puberty, frequent emotional shifts are normal in both guys and girls. Sometimes things happen to trigger changes in our emotions. Listen to the story of "The Terrible, Horrible, Super, Wonderful Day." Pretend you're the story's main character—Shawn. Each time you feel happy or positive, stand up. Then, when you hear something that makes you feel bad, sit down. You may stand and sit as many times as you want. Look around as others stand and sit during the story, but make your own decisions on when to stand or sit.**

Read the story slowly, pausing slightly when kids stand or sit.

Read aloud "The Terrible, Horrible, Super, Wonderful Day" in the margin.

Afterward, ask:

● **What did you notice about when people would stand or sit?** (We all responded the same way; some people responded differently than others.)

● **Did guys and girls stand or sit at different times? Explain.** (Yes, guys didn't stand as much for the good stuff that happened; no, they responded the same.)

● **What does that tell you about guys' and girls' emotional responses to situations?** (Guys don't show their feelings as much; guys and girls both have similar feelings.)

● **How is standing and sitting like the emotions you experience in a typical day?** (I never know how I'm going to feel from one minute to the next; sometimes I wish I wasn't so emotional.)

Say: **While guys and girls may have different ways to show emotions, they both feel the same things. The Bible can help us deal with some of those emotions in a positive way.**

The Terrible, Horrible, Super, Wonderful Day

Shawn's alarm clock startles him out of a dream promptly at 7 a.m. Still half asleep, he falls out of bed to start the day. As he gets dressed, he notices a hole in the shirt he was going to wear. With a muffled grumble, he whips off the shirt and tosses it behind him.

As he pulls another shirt from the closet, Shawn hears his dad's morning voice: "Get going. You have to walk to your bus stop today. I'm not going that way."

"Humph," sighs Shawn.

As Shawn heads downstairs, he smells his favorite breakfast cooking. He gobbles a plateful of eggs and bacon, and heads out. As he goes down the street, he runs into his best friend and they walk toward the bus together. Just before they get to the bus stop, Shawn remembers he left his homework on the kitchen table. As he runs back to get it, the bus passes by and he ends up being late for school. Since it's not the first time he's been late, his homeroom teacher sends him to the principal. He gets detention.

As Shawn leaves the principal's office, a girl he likes gives him a big smile and wishes him luck on his game after school. When he gets to his music class, he discovers he made first-chair trumpet in the jazz band. At lunch, however, he drops spaghetti on his pants and the girls at the next table start giggling and pointing.

At the football game, Shawn sees the girl who smiled at him. She's sitting in the front row of the bleachers looking right at him. He fumbles the first pass, but catches the next two. Just before halftime, he scores a touchdown. Looking up, he sees his parents cheering in the stands. He wonders how they got off work early.

When he gets home, Shawn's math teacher has left a message on the answering machine. His father blows up over Shawn's math grade and grounds him for a month.

When Shawn opens a letter from his grandparents, a $20 bill falls out. They thought he might need a little extra money for school clothes.

Shawn's favorite TV show is coming on. But he suddenly remembers he hasn't done his homework yet. As he trudges upstairs, his mother yells, "I love you. Sleep tight!"

After Shawn finishes his homework, he falls asleep dreaming of the girl with the big smile.

WHO'S AFRAID OF THE BIG BAD WOLF?

Ask for a volunteer to play the part of Jesus. With the rest of the class, form three groups. Assign one group to play the disciples. Assign another group to be the wind, and the last group to be the waves. Tell kids you're going to read Mark 4:35-41 aloud and they'll provide the action. Give kids a couple of minutes to read the passage and plan what they're going to do in the improvisational drama. Encourage groups to be dramatic and creative. The "wind" group might choose to howl like the wind. The wave group might use hand motions to simulate the movement of the waves. Anything goes!

Call the groups together and read aloud Mark 4:35-41, pausing after each sentence. As you read, have groups each improvise their part.

After the drama, congratulate kids' efforts.

Then ask:

● **How are you like the disciples in this story?** (Sometimes I wonder whether God is in control; I worry about things I can't do anything about.)

● **The disciples feared the storm would topple their boat. What kind of fears do you have?** (Afraid my parents will divorce; afraid I won't fit in.)

● **What difference can Jesus make if he rides with you in the "boat" of your life?** (He can calm the storms if I believe in him; he can make me feel safe just knowing he's there.)

Say: **Fear is a normal part of living. Often fears are more frequent during puberty because there are so many unknowns. But, like other feelings, fear is something both guys and girls have.**

Have guys and girls each describe fears they have. Then say: **Let's look at another Bible character who was faced with unknowns—Joshua.**

Form two groups. Have groups each read aloud Joshua 1:1-11. Give each group paper and a pencil. Have one group list from the passage all of God's promises to Joshua. Kids might list God's promises of a new homeland or always being with the people. Have the other group list from the passage all of God's instructions to Joshua. Kids might list instructions such as be strong and courageous; follow the law; meditate on the law.

When groups are finished, have them each explain their list.

Then ask:

● **What does this Bible passage have to do with growing up?** (God has promised to be with us too; our success in the future will depend on keeping God's law.)

● **How can these verses help both guys and girls overcome fears and other negative feelings?** (They remind us to trust God; God's promises to Joshua are true for us too.)

● **Which of God's promises to Joshua are true for you**

today? (If I follow God's teachings, I'll be successful in all I do; God will always be with us.)

Say: **God gives us lots of promises in the Bible. And believing in them helps us make good choices about our emotions. But circumstances can still influence how we feel. Let's evaluate our emotions in different situations.**

EMOTION POTIONS

Give kids each an "Emotion Potion" handout (p. 44) and a pencil. Have kids follow the instructions on the handout.

Form groups of no more than four. Have group members compare their potion jars.

Ask:

● **Why are your responses different for the same situations?** (We all have different reactions to circumstances; the situations really aren't the same.)

Form a circle. Set out a pitcher filled with water. Also set out a baking pan with an empty glass sitting in it.

Ask:

● **How far did you fill the jar labeled "When I think about the love given to me by God"?**

● **Do you think there are limits on God's love for us?** (No, he loves us unconditionally; yes, his love goes away each time we disobey him.)

Say: **Pretend this glass is an emotion potion jar. The water in the pitcher represents God's love. When I pour the water to the level you colored in on your handout, tell me to stop.**

Fill the glass with water. Instead of stopping when instructed, continue filling the glass until it overflows into the baking pan.

Say: **We put limits on God's love for us, but he wants his love to overflow in our lives. God never stops loving us. We also put limits on the kinds of emotions guys or girls should have, or how they'll show those feelings. But as we've learned today, guys and girls have similar feelings.**

Form same-sex groups of no more than four. Have groups each choose one thing they've learned about how members of the opposite sex express their feelings. For example, girls might say, "Guys may really be sad or down when they seem angry." Guys might say, "Girls get just as angry about things as guys do."

Then have groups each share what they chose with the rest of the groups. Form a circle, alternating guys and girls in the circle as much as possible. Then have kids repeat the following commitment after you read it aloud. Read one phrase at a time to make it easier for kids to repeat. Say: **I don't always understand members of the opposite sex. But they have the same feelings I do. I commit to being more sensitive to the feelings expressed by members of the opposite sex.**

Have kids each shake hands with three other people in the

COMMITMENT
(5 to 10 minutes)

room, each time telling that person one way they see God's love flow through him or her. Make sure everyone receives at least one hand shake.

☐ OPTION 1: HOW I FEEL

Give kids each a sheet of construction paper. Say: **Your feelings are important. And whether you're a guy or a girl, you'll experience lots of different feelings as you grow into adulthood. Tear or fold your construction paper to show how you feel about emotions expressed by the opposite sex. You might tear the paper into a question mark to show you don't understand. Or you may fold your paper into a heart to show you care.**

Have kids each describe their paper shape. Then form a circle and have kids place their paper shapes in the center. Have kids put their arms around each other to form a group hug. Then close in prayer, thanking God for emotions. Encourage kids to keep their paper shape for a couple of weeks to remind them to be sensitive to how members of the opposite sex are feeling.

☐ OPTION 2: HAPPY (AND SAD) TOGETHER

Say: **We've learned today that guys and girls deal with the same kinds of feelings, but people express those feelings in different ways. I'm going to call out specific feelings. When I do, act out how you or someone you know shows that feeling. For example, when I call out anger, you might stomp your feet or scream.**

Call out the following feelings:
- **Fear**
- **Sadness**
- **Anger**
- **Excitement**

Say: **I've got one more emotion for you to express. But I want it to be a true response to what I'm going to say. When I've finished speaking, express your feeling to someone near you. Ready? (Pause.) God loves you so much he sent his son to die in your place. God loves you with immeasurable love.**

CLOSING
(up to 5 minutes)

If You Still Have Time . . .

Course Reflection—Form a circle. Ask students to reflect on the past four sessions. Have them take turns completing the following sentences:
- Something I learned in this course was . . .
- If I could tell my friends about this course, I'd say . . .
- Something I'll do differently because of this course is . . .

Reaching Out—Form two teams. Have a contest to see which team can develop the most ideas for reaching out to kids who are feeling down. Share ideas and have kids each commit to doing one thing from the list this week.

Emotion Potion

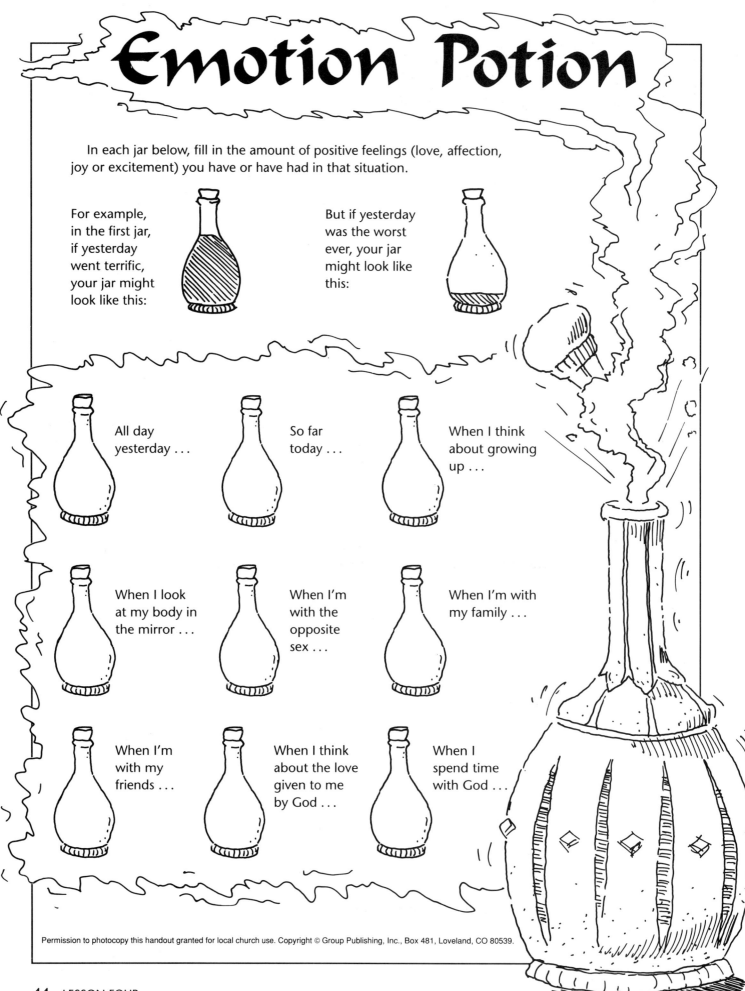

In each jar below, fill in the amount of positive feelings (love, affection, joy or excitement) you have or have had in that situation.

For example, in the first jar, if yesterday went terrific, your jar might look like this:

But if yesterday was the worst ever, your jar might look like this:

All day yesterday . . .

So far today . . .

When I think about growing up . . .

When I look at my body in the mirror . . .

When I'm with the opposite sex . . .

When I'm with my family . . .

When I'm with my friends . . .

When I think about the love given to me by God . . .

When I spend time with God . . .

BONUS IDEAS

Dear Diary—Have kids each keep a diary for one month. Have them each record their feelings, thoughts, new experiences, questions, body changes and spiritual growth. When the month is over, have a meeting centered around the diaries. Keep specific entries confidential, but have kids use their diaries to talk about trends or patterns they see. For example, kids can discuss how often their moods change or how many times they've dealt with the same troubling issue. Encourage kids to ask questions that have arisen because of the diaries.

Table Talk—Use the "Table Talk" handout (p. 20) as the basis for a meeting with parents and kids. Give each person a handout before the meeting. Open with a pop quiz about physical changes in guys and girls. See page 25 for an example of what to include. Then have parents each share with their junior higher how they first learned about puberty and what they experienced at that time.

Esteem Boosters—Use this idea to help kids build self-esteem during puberty. Provide newspapers and magazines for each person. Have kids each find articles about kids their age who are making a positive difference in their communities. Then brainstorm ways your kids can make a difference in your area. Commit to beginning one service project with your group.

Body-Image Meeting—Provide magazines and two white paper tablecloths. Have kids make giant paper dolls out of the tablecloths. Then have them tape magazine photographs on them, showing positive characteristics of men and women. When kids are finished, have kids compare their creations to their own bodies and personalities. Form a circle, and ask each person to complete a different one of these open-ended statements:
- I wish my body was less . . .
- I wish my body was more . . .
- I hate my . . .
- Other people probably think I'm . . .
- I wish I could . . .
- My personality is missing . . .
- I'm glad my personality includes . . .

Stereotype Ratings—Give kids each a "Smashing Stereotypes" handout (p. 48) and a pencil. Have kids each answer

MEETINGS AND MORE

the questions on the handout. Then explain the scoring procedures and let kids score their handouts. Have volunteers share their scores and discuss the stereotypes.

Mechanics and Nurses—Have kids create a play or skit based on the changing roles of men and women in society. The play might include characters such as a male nurse, a female auto mechanic and a female baseball umpire. Use preparation of the skit and the skit to spark discussion on appropriate roles for men and women at church, home and work.

Tell Me About It—Invite college-age guys and girls to attend a meeting with your junior highers. Have the young adults tell junior highers about the ups and downs they experienced as they went through puberty. Include discussions on understanding the opposite sex; overcoming low self-esteem; and how faith fits in with growing up.

Have kids write questions ahead of time they'd like to ask the young adults.

PARTY PLEASERS

Post-Puberty Party—Follow a birthday theme and have a Happy Birthday Adulthood party. Serve "adult" appetizers such as finger sandwiches and hot tea. Have kids dress in their parent's clothes. Have kids each complete an identification card that describes what they'll be like 15 years from now. Have kids include this information on the card:

- marital status
- children (how many)
- where I live
- career
- income
- physical appearance
- today's date
- church involvement

When kids are finished, have them each explain their card. Then have kids each wrap their card in birthday paper and keep it with them to open in 15 years. Explain that trusting God and making the best of each day now will help make kids' future dream-life come true.

Memory Lane Party—Have kids each bring their photo history (compiled from family photo albums). After kids arrive, provide posterboard, markers and tape. Have kids each create a montage using their photographs. Be sure kids are careful not to damage the photos. When everyone is finished, have kids each tell their history, using the photos as needed. Then discuss ways God has been with kids since they were children. Explain that God's Holy Spirit stays with Christians to help them through hard times—even puberty—and through the hard times, he helps them become more like Jesus.

Wow! Look at Me Now Retreat—Have a puberty retreat. Lead sessions on physiological changes, fluctuating feelings, daring dates, premarital sex, and masturbation. Have an anonymous question box, and answer all questions possible. You may want to have a few sessions separating guys and girls.

Tic-Tac-Toe Lock-In—Have a wild lock-in filled with favorite childhood games. Between games, conduct "timeline talks." Ask kids about their earliest memories, their favorite childhood activities, their first day at school and their hobbies. Then do a Bible study on Mark 10:13-16. When the lights go out for bedtime, play lullabies to put everyone to sleep.

SMASHING STEREOTYPES

LINCOLN CHRISTIAN COLLEGE AND SEMINARY

Read each sentence and decide how you feel about it. Circle the answer that matches your feelings.

A=Agree   D=Disagree

A D   1. Women should have the freedom to have a career if they want.

A D   2. Men make good secretaries and nurses.

A D   3. Women shouldn't be physically strong.

A D   4. Men shouldn't cry.

A D   5. Men who stay at home while their wives work are lazy.

A D   6. If a husband and wife both work, the wife should do most of the cooking and cleaning.

A D   7. Men can be as good with children as women are.

A D   8. Women should make the decisions in their families.

A D   9. It's more important for teenage guys to have jobs since they pay for the dates.

A D   10. Only women can take care of the household and cook the meals.

A D   11. Guys know how to share their feelings as well as girls.

A D   12. Husbands should help their wives cook, clean house and do laundry.

A D   13. It's okay for guys to have sex before marriage.

A D   14. Women can do most things men can do.

A D   15. Men can do most things women can do.

Scoring

For every "A" on statements 3-6, 8-10 and 13, give yourself 3 points. For every "D" on questions 1-2, 7, 11-12 and 14-15, give yourself 3 points.

0 to 9 points—Congratulations! You're not sexist!
12 to 15 points—Watch out! You may have stereotyped thoughts.
18 points and up—You need to seriously re-evaluate the way you see the opposite sex.